The Dialogue of the Savior

*Mystical Conversations on
Divine Truth and Enlightenment*

A Modern Translation

Adapted for the Contemporary Reader

**Anonymous
(Gnostic Tradition, 2nd Century CE)**

Translated by Tim Zengerink

© Copyright 2025
All rights reserved.

It is not legal to reproduce, duplicate, or transmit any part of this document in either electronic means or in printed format. Recording of this publication is strictly prohibited and any storage of this document is not allowed unless with written permission from the publisher except for the use of brief quotations in a book review.

This book contains works of fiction. Any resemblance to persons living or dead, or places, events, or locations is purely coincidental.

Table Of Contents

Preface - Message to the Reader 1

Introduction 5

Dialogue of The Savior 10

Thank You for Reading 27

Preface - Message to the Reader

What If You Could Help Rebuild the Greatest Library in Human History?

Thousands of years ago, the Library of Alexandria stood as the crown jewel of human achievement — a sanctuary where the collected wisdom of every known civilization was gathered, preserved, and shared freely.

And then, it was lost.

Through fire, conquest, and the slow erosion of time, humanity lost not just books — but ideas, dreams, discoveries, and stories that could have changed the world forever.

Today, the Library of Alexandria lives again — and you are invited to be a part of its restoration.

Our mission is simple yet profound:

To rebuild the greatest library the world has ever known, and to translate all timeless works into every language and dialect, so that no seeker of knowledge is ever left behind again.

By joining our movement to rebuild the modern Library of Alexandria, you become part of an unprecedented mission:

- **Unlimited Access to the Greatest Audiobooks & eBooks Ever Written:**

  Instantly explore thousands of legendary works—Plato, Shakespeare, Jane Austen, Leo Tolstoy, and countless more. All instantly available to read or listen, placing a complete literary universe at your fingertips.

- **Beautiful Paperback & Deluxe Editions at Printing Cost**

  Own any title as an elegant paperback, deluxe hardcover, or stunning collectible boxset—offered to you at true printing cost, delivered straight to your door. Build your personal Library of Alexandria, crafted for beauty, built for durability, and worthy of proud display.

- **Fresh Translations for Modern Readers—in Every Language & Dialect**

  Enjoy timeless masterpieces reimagined in clear, contemporary language—no more outdated phrases or obscure references. Alongside the original versions, we're tirelessly translating these classics into every language and dialect imaginable, ensuring accessibility and understanding across cultures and generations.

- **Join a Global Renaissance of Literature & Knowledge**

  You directly support expanding our library, publishing deluxe editions at true cost, translating works into all global languages, and bringing humanity's greatest stories to people everywhere. By joining today, you're not just preserving a legacy of masterpieces; you set in motion a powerful wave of literary accessibility.

Become a Torchbearer of Knowledge.

Join us for free now at **LibraryofAlexandria.com**

Together, we will ensure that the light of human wisdom never fades again.

With gratitude and a shared love of knowledge,

The Modern Library of Alexandria Team

Visit:

www.libraryofalexandria.com

Or scan the code below:

Introduction

Divine Conversation and the Search for Truth

The Dialogue of the Savior stands as one of the most intricate and spiritually resonant works within the Gnostic tradition. Unearthed among the texts of the Nag Hammadi library, this enigmatic gospel departs from traditional narrative structures and enters instead into the realm of sacred conversation. At its core, this work presents an extended dialogue between the risen Savior and his disciples—Mary, Matthew, Judas, and others—on the nature of truth, the soul's path to liberation, and the mysteries of existence that transcend the material world.

What distinguishes The Dialogue of the Savior from other apocryphal or canonical gospels is its philosophical intensity and meditative tone. The text does not follow a linear progression of events, but unfolds as a series of questions and answers—each response leading not to finality, but to deeper reflection. The disciples ask not for miracles, but for meaning. They do not seek authority, but understanding. Their inquiries echo the universal questions of the soul: What is truth? What is the nature of the divine? How do we return to the realm of light from which we came?

The Savior's responses are poetic, symbolic, and often paradoxical. He speaks of the inner light, the necessity of stillness, the limitations of the body, and the deceptive nature of the material world. His teachings call not for obedience but for insight—not for faith in dogma, but for awakening to inner knowledge. The goal is not to please an external deity but to remember the divine origin of the soul and reclaim the path of ascent. This is the heart of Gnostic soteriology: salvation through self-knowledge, liberation through recognition, enlightenment through gnosis.

The conversation in the text is deeply intimate, as though overheard in a quiet room rather than proclaimed to crowds. There is no thunderous sermon, no elaborate ritual. Instead, there is presence: the quiet, sacred act of speaking and listening with full attention. In this way, The Dialogue of the Savior reflects a different vision of the spiritual teacher. The Savior is not distant or imperious. He is near, compassionate, and entirely devoted to the awakening of those who are ready. He guides not with laws, but with wisdom; not with demands, but with insight.

This approach aligns with the broader Gnostic worldview. For Gnostics, the divine is not primarily a judge or king, but a source of light hidden within. The world we see is not the full reality—it is a shadow, a distortion crafted by lower powers. The Demiurge, the architect of this material world, is a being of ignorance who believes himself to be the highest god. Against this illusion, the true Savior enters—not to overthrow, but to illuminate. He comes to remind the soul of what it has forgotten and to guide it back to its origin in the realm of fullness (pleroma).

The Soul's Ascent and the Wisdom of Silence

A major theme running through The Dialogue of the Savior is the ascent of the soul. The disciples learn that the soul is not created for the material world. It is a sojourner, a traveler in exile. The body, while necessary for experience, is not the soul's home. It is a garment, a temporary vessel. The true self is not what can be seen, touched, or named—it is the divine spark, the immortal essence that belongs to the Light.

Yet the journey back is not simple. The soul must contend with layers of illusion, forgetfulness, and resistance. The Savior teaches that fear and ignorance are the greatest obstacles. The soul must pass through the realms of the archons—the cosmic rulers who enforce ignorance. It must learn to recognize its own nature, to transcend desire, and to resist the seductive pull of falsehood. This is not a call to escape the world entirely, but to see through it—to live in it without being of it.

The path requires inner transformation, not outer conformity. The Savior speaks of silence, stillness, and reflection. These are not passive states, but active disciplines. In silence, the soul hears what noise conceals. In stillness, it moves inward toward the truth. The Savior teaches that enlightenment is not found in temples or texts alone, but in the heart that is open and the mind that is ready. This is why much of the teaching is given through metaphor and symbol. The truth is not handed to the seeker—it is awakened in them.

Among the disciples, Mary emerges as a particularly insightful figure. She asks penetrating questions and receives profound responses. Her presence in the dialogue reflects the Gnostic elevation of spiritual equality and the acknowledgment of the feminine as a bearer of wisdom. In contrast to some later orthodox traditions that marginalized female voices, The Dialogue of the Savior affirms that spiritual insight is not determined by gender, status, or hierarchy. It is a matter of receptivity, longing, and inner clarity.

This modern translation aims to preserve the meditative tone, symbolic richness, and philosophical precision of the original text. Archaic or obscure expressions have been clarified, but the poetic structure and spiritual nuance have been retained. The text is meant to be read slowly, aloud if possible, allowing the rhythm of the dialogue to unfold like a prayer. Each question is an invitation. Each answer is a doorway. The reader is not a passive observer but a participant in the conversation.

To engage with The Dialogue of the Savior is to enter a sacred encounter. It is to sit with those first seekers and listen for the voice of wisdom. It is to hear the echoes of one's own questions in their words, and to recognize one's own journey in their searching. This is not merely a historical text—it is a living guide. Its truth is not in propositions, but in presence. It does not speak from above, but from within.

Let this book be your companion in the quest for truth. Let the Savior's voice stir your memory. Let the silence between the lines awaken your own knowing. For in seeking truth, you seek yourself. And in finding yourself, you return to the Light from which you came.

Dialogue of The Savior

The Savior said to his disciples, "My brothers, the time has come for us to step away from our work and find rest. Those who find true rest will stay in it forever. I tell you, rise above the worries of this world. Do not be afraid, even when fear and anger seem to grow around you. Many before you have heard these teachings with fear, placing themselves under rulers who offered them nothing in return. But when I came, I opened the way and showed you a path that only those who are chosen and walk alone—those who know the Father and believe in the truth—can follow.

"Give thanks, for when you praise, you honor the Father. When you offer your praise, say these words:

Hear us, Father, just as you heard your only Son. You received him and gave him peace beyond this world. You are the source of power, light, and life. You are the giver of wisdom and peace to those who walk alone. Hear us, just as you heard those you have chosen. Through your gift, they enter your kingdom. Through their good works, they free themselves from the blindness of this world and find eternal life. Amen.

"I will teach you. When the time of destruction comes, the first force of darkness will rise. Do not be afraid or believe that this is the end. When you see a single staff appear, know its meaning. The rulers will come for you, and fear will try to take hold of you. But do not let fear control you, for they will not spare or show mercy to anyone. Instead, stay focused on the truth. You have learned the ways of this world, and that wisdom will lead you beyond the reach of tyrants. When you reach that place, you will meet those who came before you, and they will guide you with reason and truth.

"Move through the fearful passage with a steady mind. It is deep and overwhelming, but if you stay focused, you will pass through it. Flames and forces may rise against you, but they cannot defeat you. Remember, you are not tied to this world or its darkness. You hold the truth, and through it, you will find joy and light."

Matthew asked, "What will still exist when everything else is gone?"

The Savior answered, "The truth within you will remain. That is eternal."

Judas asked, "Lord, what will happen to the souls of those who are small and humble? Where will their spirits go?"

The Lord said, "They will be received. These souls do not die or disappear because they have known their purpose and the one who welcomes them. The truth searches for those who are wise and righteous."

The Savior said, "The lamp of the body is the mind. When your inner self is clear and in order, your whole body is filled with light. But when your heart is dark, the light you expect will not come. I have taught you this, and I send my word with you."

His disciples asked, "Lord, who is the one who searches, and who is the one who reveals?"

The Lord answered, "The one who searches is also the one who reveals."

Matthew asked, "When I speak, who listens, and who reveals?"

The Lord said, "The one who speaks is the one who listens. The one who sees is the one who reveals."

Mary asked, "Lord, why do I feel both sorrow and joy in my body?"

The Lord answered, "The body feels sorrow because of its actions, but the mind finds joy in the spirit. If someone does not understand darkness, they cannot fully see the light. Darkness hides the truth, but light reveals it. Stay close to the light, for it will last forever."

Judas asked, "Lord, what existed before the heavens and the earth?"

The Lord said, "There was darkness and water, and the spirit moved above it. Within you lies the power and mystery of that same spirit. Search within yourself, for the answers are already in your mind."

Another disciple asked, "Lord, where is the place of truth, and where does the true mind live?"

The Lord answered, "The fire of the spirit created both. From this fire, truth and the mind were formed. If someone lifts their soul, they will rise higher."

Matthew asked, "Who has the strength to guide others and overcome the forces of this world?"

The Lord said, "The one who knows their own heart and follows it with honesty will overcome both the powers above and the powers below. Those who have power should release it and turn back to the truth. Seek, find, and rejoice in what is real."

Judas said, "I see that everything in life is like signs written on something. Is that why things happen the way they do?"

The Lord replied, "When the Father created the universe, he separated the waters from it, and his Word went out, filling many places. It rose higher than the paths that surround the earth and hovered over the gathered waters. Around these waters was a great wall of fire. In time, many things took shape from what was inside.

"When the universe was complete, the Father looked at it and said, 'Go and bring forth life so that nothing will be missing from one generation to the next, from age to age.' And the universe gave freely—fountains of milk and honey, oil and wine, fruits and sweet scents, and roots of goodness. It shared everything so that nothing would ever run out. Above all, it stood in beauty, surrounded by a powerful light. No other light could compare, for it ruled over all things, above and below. Fire spread from it, moving upward and downward, and everything depended on it—both the heavens above and the earth below."

When Judas heard this, he bowed down and praised the Lord.

Mary turned to her brothers and said, "Where will you keep these teachings that you ask the Son about?"

The Lord said to her, "Sister, only those who are open in their hearts can understand these things. They must prepare themselves to receive what is coming so they won't be trapped by the limitations of this world."

Matthew asked, "Lord, I want to see the place of true life, where there is no evil, only pure light!"

The Lord said, "Brother Matthew, as long as you are in your physical body, you cannot see it."

Matthew replied, "Lord, even if I cannot see it, can you help me understand it?"

The Lord said, "Anyone who truly understands themselves will find it in all they do. They will recognize it through their own goodness."

Judas asked, "Lord, what causes the earth to shake?"

The Lord picked up a stone and held it in his hand. "What am I holding?" he asked.

Judas answered, "A stone."

The Lord said, "What holds the earth together is the same as what holds the heavens. When the Word comes from the Great Power, it supports both heaven and earth. The earth does not move on its own; if it did, it would fall. But it stays steady because the First Word does not fail. This Word created the universe, filled it, and gave it its beauty. Everything that remains still is connected to you, the children of humankind. You come from that place. You exist in the hearts of those who speak with joy and truth. Even if the Word appears in the body of the Father and is not received, it will still return to its place.

"Those who do not understand perfection understand nothing. Without knowing darkness, one cannot fully see the light. If someone does not know where fire comes from, they will be burned by it. If they do not understand the purpose of water, their baptism is meaningless. If they do not know where the wind comes from, they will be carried away by it. In the same way, if someone does not understand their own body, they will perish with it. How can someone who does not know the Son truly know the Father? To those who do not know the root of all things, everything remains hidden. Those who do not understand evil are caught in it. And those who do not know where they came from will not know where they are going, lost in a world that will eventually fade away."

The Lord then led Judas, Matthew, and Mary to the edge of heaven and earth. He placed his hand on them, and they longed to understand what they saw. Judas looked up and saw an incredibly high place, and below, a deep abyss. He said to Matthew, "Brother, who could ever climb so high or go down into that depth? The fire there is overwhelming and terrifying!"

At that moment, a Word came from above. Judas saw it descend and asked, "Why have you come down?"

The Son of Man greeted them and said, "A seed from a great power fell short and sank into the depths of the earth. The Great Power remembered it and sent the Word to retrieve it, bringing it back so that the First

Word would not fail."

The disciples were amazed at all he had revealed to them. They believed his words and realized that wickedness had no value.

The Lord said, "Did I not tell you that the good will rise into the light as quickly as lightning?"

The disciples praised him, saying, "Lord, before you came, who gave you praise? For all praise exists because of you. Who could bless you? For all blessings come from you."

As they stood there, they saw two spirits carrying a soul, surrounded by a great flash of light. A Word came from the Son of Man, saying, "Give them their garment!" The small one became like the great one, and they became one. The disciples marveled at what they saw.

Mary asked, "How can we recognize evil when it tries to hide?"

The Lord said, "When it grows large, it will reveal itself. But when you see the One Who Always Exists, you will witness the great vision."

They asked, "Tell us about it!"

He said, "Do you want to see it as something temporary or something eternal? Seek to save what will last beyond you. Search for it, speak from within it, and bring all things into harmony. The living God is within you, just as you dwell in Him."

Judas said, "I want to truly understand."

The Lord replied, "Life itself exists in everything, even in what is incomplete."

Judas asked, "But the rulers above us—won't they have power over us?"

The Lord said, "No, you will rule over them. But only when you free yourselves from jealousy. Then you will be clothed in light and enter the place of union."

Judas asked, "How will we receive our garments?"

The Lord said, "Some will give them to you, and others will receive from you. They are the ones who will bring you your garments. Who among you can truly reach the place of reward? The garments of life were given to humanity because they understand the path to leave this world. Yet even for me, it is difficult to reach."

Mary said, "This reminds me of 'the struggles of each day,' 'the worker is worthy of their food,' and 'the student will become like the teacher.'" She spoke with understanding and wisdom.

The disciples asked, "What is completeness, and what is lacking?"

He answered, "You come from completeness, but you live in a place that is lacking. But look—his light has poured out upon me!"

Matthew asked, "Lord, how do the dead die, and how do the living live?"

The Lord said, "You have asked about a deep truth that no eye has seen, nor ear has heard—except through you. I tell you, when what gives life to a person departs, they are called 'dead.' And when the living are called, they will rise."

Judas asked, "Then why do people die and live again for the sake of truth?"

The Lord said, "Anything that comes from truth cannot die. But anything born from a woman will die."

Mary asked, "Lord, why am I here? Is it to gain something or to lose?"

The Lord said, "You show the abundance of the one who reveals."

Mary asked, "Lord, is there a place where truth does not exist?"

The Lord answered, "Truth is missing only in places where I am not."

Mary said, "Lord, you are both amazing and mysterious. What happens to those who do not know you?"

Matthew asked, "Why don't we find rest right away?"

The Lord replied, "You will rest when you let go of the burdens you carry."

Matthew asked, "How can something small become part of something great?"

The Lord said, "When you let go of things that cannot follow you, you will find rest."

Mary said, "I want to understand everything exactly as it is!"

The Lord said, "Seek true life, for that is real wealth. The riches of this world—gold and silver—are only illusions."

The disciples asked, "How can we make our work perfect?"

The Lord said, "Be prepared for anything. Blessed is the one who faces the struggle, who neither harms nor is harmed, but comes out victorious."

Judas asked, "What is the first step on the right path?"

The Lord said, "Love and kindness. If the rulers had these, evil would have never existed."

Matthew said, "Lord, you talk about the end of all things without fear."

The Lord said, "You have listened to my words and believed them. If you truly understand them, they belong to you. If not, they are not yours yet."

The disciples asked, "Where should we go?"

The Lord answered, "Go as far as you can."

Mary said, "Everything that is meant to happen is already seen."

The Lord said, "It is the one who sees who brings revelation."

The twelve disciples asked, "Teacher, tell us about peace."

The Lord said, "Everything I have shown you, you will understand. In time, it will all become clear."

Mary said, "Lord, there is one truth I will share with you: we exist in full view of the universe."

Judas said to Matthew, "We want to understand what kind of clothes we will wear when we leave behind our physical bodies."

The Lord said, "The rulers and their servants wear clothes that do not last. But as children of truth, you will not wear such temporary garments. Instead, you will be blessed when you remove them, because it is no great thing to let go of what is only on the outside."

Mary asked, "What is the mustard seed? Is it something heavenly or something earthly?"

The Lord said, "When the Father created the universe, He left much behind from the Mother of All. From this, He speaks and acts."

Judas asked, "You speak from truth. How should we pray?"

The Lord said, "Pray in a place where there is no woman."

Matthew explained, "He means to 'remove the works of womanhood,' not because birth happens in any other way, but because birth itself will one day end."

Mary said, "Birth will never stop."

The Lord said, "Who truly knows that it won't?"

Judas said to Matthew, "The works of womanhood will come to an end, and the rulers will lose their power. This is how we will prepare."

The Lord said, "That's right. Do the rulers see you? Do they see those who receive you? A true Word is coming from the Father to the depths, in silence and as fast as lightning, bringing forth life. Do they see it or have power over it? But you understand this path better than any angel or authority ever has. This path belongs to the Father and the Son because they are one. You will walk this path that you already know. Even if the rulers become powerful, they cannot reach it. I tell you, even for me, it is difficult to reach."

Mary asked, "When things dissolve, what happens to what they created?"

The Lord said, "They return to their proper place, just as they were meant to."

Judas asked, "How is the spirit revealed?"

The Lord said, "How is a sword revealed?"

Judas asked, "How does light appear?"

The Lord said, "[...] in it forever."

Judas continued, "Who forgives whose actions? Which actions in the world are forgiven, and who has the power to forgive them?"

The Lord replied, "Whoever understands these actions must follow the will of the Father. As for you, work to remove anger and jealousy from your hearts. Let go of the things that weigh you down and keep you from the truth. [...] Whoever frees themselves from these burdens will live forever. I tell you this so that you do not lead your spirit and soul into confusion."

Paul, an apostle, not appointed by men nor through human authority, but by Jesus Christ, writes to the brothers in Laodicea:

Grace and peace to you from God the Father and the Lord Jesus Christ.

I always thank Christ in my prayers for you, hoping

that you stay strong in Him, faithful to His teachings, and always looking forward to the promise of the final day of judgment.

Do not be distracted by empty words—words from those who try to deceive you and lead you away from the truth of the Gospel that I have preached to you.

God will ensure that those who stand with me continue to share the truth of the Gospel, bringing goodness and salvation that leads to eternal life.

My imprisonment for Christ is clear to everyone, yet I find joy and peace in it.

For me, this is eternal salvation, made possible by your prayers and the guidance of the Holy Spirit, whether in life or in death.

My life belongs to Christ, and even in death, there is victory.

May His mercy work within you so that you may live in love and unity.

Dearly loved ones, as I told you when I was with you, stay strong and live in reverence for God, for it will lead you to eternal life.

For God is at work within you.

Do all things without doubt or hesitation.

And finally, rejoice in Christ and stay away from

those who are greedy and corrupt.

Bring all your concerns to God in prayer, and remain steady in the mind of Christ.

Hold on to everything that is good, true, just, and worthy of love.

Keep close to your heart what you have heard and received.

Peace will be with you.

The saints send their greetings.

May the grace of the Lord Jesus Christ be with your spirit.

Make sure that this letter is read to those in Colossae, just as their letter is to be read to you.

Brothers and sisters, as followers of the Lord, we must keep God's commandments. Those who live by His teachings will have eternal life, while those who reject them will bring destruction upon themselves and face the second death.

The Lord's command is this: Do not swear falsely. Do not steal. Do not commit adultery. Do not lie or give false testimony. Do not take bribes to cover up the truth or misuse power for injustice.

Anyone who holds power but denies the truth will be denied entry into the kingdom of God and will be cast into hell, from which there is no escape.

How weak and dishonest we are as sinners! Instead of turning away from sin daily, we continue to add sin upon sin.

Know this, beloved brothers and sisters: our actions will be recorded as evidence against us on the day of judgment. There will be no witnesses, no accomplices, and no bribery in that judgment.

Faith, truth, self-discipline, fasting, and charity are more powerful than all sins and will erase their weight.

Treat others as you wish to be treated.

Seek the kingdom of God, and you will receive the crown of life through Christ Jesus our Lord.

Thank You for Reading

Dear Reader,

We hope this timeless classic has sparked your imagination and enriched your literary journey. Now that you've turned the final page, we want to share a vision for the future of reading—one where every classic you've ever wanted to explore is at your fingertips, in a format that best suits your life.

We'd like to invite you to gain immediate, unlimited digital & audiobook access to hundreds of the most treasured literary classics ever written—along with the option to secure deluxe paperback, hardcover & box set editions at printing cost. Together, we can spark a new global literary renaissance alongside our small, independent publishing house called "The Library of Alexandria."

Thousands of years ago, the Library of Alexandria stood as a beacon of knowledge—until it was lost to history. We aim to reignite that spirit of preservation and discovery right now, in the modern age—only this time, it's accessible to all, in every language and every format.

Picture a world where every timeless classic, novel, poem, or philosophical treatise is not only available to read but also updated for today's readers—modernized, translated into any language or dialect, and ready to enjoy in any format you choose, whether that is in an eBook, audiobook, paperback, or deluxe hardcover & box set version a printing cost.

By joining our movement to rebuild the modern Library of Alexandria, you become part of an unprecedented mission to offer:

- **Unlimited Audiobook & eBook Access to the Greatest Classics of All Time**

    Instantly explore thousands of legendary works, from Plato and Shakespeare to Jane Austen and Leo Tolstoy. All are instantly ready to read or listen to, giving you a complete literary universe at your fingertips.

- **Paperback & Deluxe Editions at Printing Costs:**

    Purchase any title in a paperback, deluxe hardbound, or deluxe boxset edition at printing costs, shipped right to your doorstep. Curate your personal library of Alexandria with editions worthy of display—crafted to last, designed to captivate, and delivered straight to your door.

- **Modern translations for Contemporary Readers in all languages and dialects**

  Discover a vast selection of classics reimagined in clear, current language—no more struggling with outdated phrases or obscure references. Next to the original versions, we aim to offer translations in as many languages and dialects as possible.

  As we continue our translation efforts and add new languages, readers everywhere can connect with these works as if they were written today. By bridging linguistic divides, you're contributing to ensuring that these timeless stories become more meaningful, accessible, and inspiring for people across the globe.

- **Your Personal Library of Alexandria:**

  Over the months and years, you'll curate a unique physical archive of classics—each volume a testament to your taste, curiosity, and love of knowledge. It's not just about owning books—it's about curating a cultural legacy you'll cherish and pass down for generations to come.

- **Join a Global Literary Renaissance:**

  Your support fuels an ongoing mission: allowing us to reinvest in offering deluxe print editions (including special boxsets) at their true cost, broaden the range of available formats and translations, and extend the reach of these works to new audiences worldwide. By joining today, you're not just preserving a legacy of masterpieces; you set in motion a powerful wave of literary accessibility.

We are more than a publisher—we're a movement, and we can't do it alone. Your support lets us scale our mission, preserving and reimagining history's greatest works for tomorrow's readers.

Become a Torchbearer of knowledge.

Thank you for picking up this book and allowing us into your literary journey. As you turn the pages, know that you're part of something larger: a global effort to keep these stories alive, share their wisdom across borders and generations, and spark a true cultural revival for the modern era.

If this resonates with you—please consider taking the next step by visiting:

www.libraryofalexandria.com

With gratitude and a shared love of knowledge,

The Modern Library of Alexandria Team

Visit:

www.libraryofalexandria.com

Or scan the code below:

www.ingramcontent.com/pod-product-compliance
Lightning Source LLC
LaVergne TN
LVHW030636080426
835512LV00022B/3476